Alexis & Company
Atlanta, GA, USA
www.AlexisAndCompany.com
@CoverGirlAlexis
#WhenDreamsFeelPastDue

info@AlexisAndCompany.com
Horace.p.publishing@gmail.com

ISBN 13: 978-0-692-15663-6

ISBN 10: 0-692-15663-1

When Dreams Feel Past Due

When Dreams Feel Past Due
By
Alexis Harris

Horace P. Publishing ©
Copyright © 2018 by Alexis Harris
Illustrations by Frederick B. Reese Jr.

When Dreams Feel Past Due

All rights reserved. No part of this publication may be reproduced, distributed, or transmitted in any form or by any means, including photocopying, recording, or other electronic or mechanical methods, without the prior written permission of the author, except in the case of brief quotations embodied in critical reviews and certain other noncommercial uses permitted by copyright law. For permission requests, write to the publisher, addressed "Attention: Permissions Coordinator," at info@AlexisAndCompany.com.

Ordering Information: Quantity sales. Special discounts are available on quantity purchases by corporations, associations, and others. For details, contact the publisher at the address above.
Orders by U.S. trade bookstores and wholesalers. Please visit www.AlexisAndCompany.com.

Alexis Harris

To those who came before me,
I honor you.
To those who came after me,
I stand with you.
To those who have yet to come,
I wish you strength for the journey ahead.

When Dreams Feel Past Due

The birthing of a dream is
particularly laborious because
you could very well be in the
delivery room for years.

Alexis Harris

It takes guts to conceive dreams
in your spirit knowing your
soul will instantly fall in
love with something your
body may never birth.

When Dreams Feel Past Due

Contents

First Comes Love.... 10

Then Comes Marriage....97

Then Comes A Baby....149

In a Baby Carriage....168

Alexis Harris

When Dreams Feel Past Due

When Dreams Feel Past Due

FIRST COMES LOVE

Alexis Harris

Take note as the candle
warms her own body by
lighting the way for
others.

When Dreams Feel Past Due

The danger of putting your
life on a timeline is you'll
convince yourself events
are past due when they're
actually right on schedule.

Alexis Harris

Even though the Sun sets,
she will undoubtedly rise
again in the morning—you
are the Sun.

When Dreams Feel Past Due

The richness of my skin
reflects soil that nourishes
ecosystems and night skies
that house
galaxies.

Alexis Harris

Today the wind danced
through my hair, the
Sun massaged my
skin, and the
leaves whispered
sweet nothings
to my ears.

When Dreams Feel Past Due

My hair is my crown
and my body beneath
it is an entire castle.

Alexis Harris

All the butterflies giggled
in the walls of my abdomen
as their wings tickled my womb
causing my belly to burst into
laughter. That's when the blood
in my veins rushed to front row
seats positioned on the edge of
my fingertips—causing the stadium
of my skin to scream in sheer
excitement.

-It's Time

When Dreams Feel Past Due

The wheatgrass waved and
the Sun smiled as the wind
carried me ahead.

Alexis Harris

My soul hoped it would
be worth it. My heart
knew it would be.

When Dreams Feel Past Due

I said it before I saw it
because I knew it was
coming.

Alexis Harris

I hear compliments and
give myself permission to
both believe and accept them.

When Dreams Feel Past Due

My scars tell the stories
my makeup is too insecure
to reveal.

Alexis Harris

Don't be so hard on yourself;
you are but a spirit who
journeys an unknown
universe on a trajectory
that is uniquely
yours.

When Dreams Feel Past Due

A whirlpool of emotions
flooded my mind and I
stayed afloat by using
my smile as a life vest.

Alexis Harris

The magic in you is a gift—
use your powers for good.

When Dreams Feel Past Due

You're never too
young or too old
to experience life.

Alexis Harris

If love could be
bought, I'd still
give mine for free.

When Dreams Feel Past Due

Love—real love, good love,
real good love—is priceless.

Alexis Harris

Suffering on a timeline is
bearable; suffering indefinitely
is much harder to bear.

-How Much Longer

When Dreams Feel Past Due

Every time
my soul whispers
"just a little while longer"
my heart ends up
in the intensive
care unit.

-Hope Deferred

Alexis Harris

I was too devastated
to drink water but too
weak to stop the tears
from falling into my
mouth.

When Dreams Feel Past Due

Life must grind its
teeth, roll its eyes,
and clinch its fists
in frustration of its
own irony—for when
I asked questions, its
mouth went numb;
when I needed to see a sign,
its lids French kissed one
another; and when I begged
for a hand, its fingers
intertwined so intimately
I was sure they belonged
together.

Alexis Harris

My soul threatened to
abandon me if forced
to endure another test.
Promise me this is the
real deal.

When Dreams Feel Past Due

My bones ached attempting
to mimic my heart.

Alexis Harris

Trying to stop
yourself
from crying
is undeniably
cruel, as it
strips your
soul of the
opportunity
to purge.

When Dreams Feel Past Due

My heart was my mind's
designated driver
but soon became
drunk in love.

Alexis Harris

I popped my pimples
to punish them for
existing.

When Dreams Feel Past Due

Air filled my lungs, so I cringed
and exhaled as quickly as I could.
It returned even quicker and
promised it always would.

Alexis Harris

When you feel the need to
cry uncontrollably for reasons
unknown, do it.

When Dreams Feel Past Due

Like a sponge, you must
allow your heart to soak in
the love and squeeze out the
tears.

-Spring Cleaning

Alexis Harris

I cut her and she came back;
I poisoned her but she refused
to die; I burned her—
still, she knew no defeat;
perhaps I refuse to
let her flourish because
she's stronger than
I'll ever be.

When Dreams Feel Past Due

My body rids itself
of waste as my soul
watches in jealousy.

Alexis Harris

I begged my heart
not to give out on me;
it begged the same
in return.

-The Feeling's Mutual

When Dreams Feel Past Due

I wanted to be just
like you until I
realized you were
just like me.

Alexis Harris

You aren't magical;
you are magic.

When Dreams Feel Past Due

I was lenient to my body
when she begged to rest.
But when my mind begged
the same, I denied her
request.

Alexis Harris

When you get
tired of dreaming,
it's okay to go to sleep
for a moment—
your dreams will
renew themselves
as you renew
yourself.

When Dreams Feel Past Due

My tragedy doesn't look
like yours but it hurts
the same.

Alexis Harris

The pain taunted my
body by lingering;
so my body
retaliated
by bleeding.

When Dreams Feel Past Due

As a tree absorbs rain
to enable growth,
so too does my skin
absorb tears.

Alexis Harris

My life is not my own;
I did not create myself—
thus, I cannot end myself.
That would be theft and
I am no criminal.

When Dreams Feel Past Due

Our ability to empathize
is by intentional design,
not random chance.

Alexis Harris

Sometimes I wish you would
look away so I can do bad things.

When Dreams Feel Past Due

I've never been hopeless;
though I've slowly begun
to hope less.

Alexis Harris

It is imperative that you
exercise your right to
take care of
yourself.

When Dreams Feel Past Due

Tomorrow will come
whether we're
ready or not.

Alexis Harris

Just because you created
the problem for yourself
doesn't make it any less
of a problem.

When Dreams Feel Past Due

I despised how flawed
I was before realizing
my flaws are what
unifies me with humanity
and distinguishes me from her.

Alexis Harris

Sometimes my feelings get so hurt
over the tiniest things; still, I allow
my soul to express her grief.

When Dreams Feel Past Due

Don't wonder;
wander.

Alexis Harris

It's easy to want
to be accepted, but
not easy to accept.

When Dreams Feel Past Due

With every conversation, my
eyes draw curtains denying any
glimpse into the windows of my soul.
My blood cells run frantically down
the aisles of my arteries, while my
veins catch a train to my heart;
forcing me to engage in small talk.

-Anxious for Nothing

Alexis Harris

I used to wish
I could keep it
together all the time;
then the wishing
well disappeared.

When Dreams Feel Past Due

Don't tell me to
relax—tell me
it's taken care of.

Alexis Harris

We aren't meant
to be idols—
we're spirits;
and far too
fragile to be tied
down to other
people's desires.

When Dreams Feel Past Due

We're told birth
is beautiful;
but taught to
despise the
stretch marks.

Alexis Harris

My cellulite is not
your problem;
in fact, it's not
a problem at all.

When Dreams Feel Past Due

Love spelled backwards is evol;
love lived backwards is evil.

Alexis Harris

The ones who roll with the
punches avoid being
knocked out.

When Dreams Feel Past Due

Chasing dreams is exhausting;
learn to function exhausted.

Alexis Harris

Speak your truth;
for it is worth
hearing.

When Dreams Feel Past Due

Snap out of it;
you're doing much
better than you
think you are.

Alexis Harris

Why are we so quick to judge?
Who do we think we are?
Every nip, every tuck
leaves a fresh new scar.
Not on me, of course,
I can handle my own.
But on those trying to
please you; those with an
invisible backbone.

You try to make us and
mold us into who
you want us to be:
*tone your legs, lift your butt
it only takes a little surgery.*
Then you'll be perfect—
you'll be everything
I want you to be.

Well, I got a solution
to your problem whether
you take heed or can't;
my so-called-problems
are subjective and superficial
but you, my dear, need
a heart transplant.

When Dreams Feel Past Due

I used to despise
mean people
now I pity them.
For I've never
known utter
misery but
they appear
to know her
so well.

Alexis Harris

I truly began living
when I realized control
was both overrated
and impractical.

When Dreams Feel Past Due

We're born with
everything we need
but told it's not
enough.
It is.

Alexis Harris

Never be afraid to
say "no." But
don't forget to
say yes, too.

When Dreams Feel Past Due

I bite my tongue
because it's better
than biting you.

Alexis Harris

My strength evolved with
time and continues to
evolve over time.

When Dreams Feel Past Due

Refuse to believe this is
where your story ends
and start writing your
next chapter.

Alexis Harris

I am in no way, shape, or
form ever responsible for
your actions.

When Dreams Feel Past Due

All paths are temporary
and capable of being changed—
never let anyone convince you
otherwise.

Alexis Harris

The Sun sent her rays
to warm my body; my
body promised to send
the warmth back.

When Dreams Feel Past Due

Veins climb the walls of my
body like vines wrapping
themselves around my
heart—reminding me
that I am alive, indeed.

Alexis Harris

If you listen closely,
you'll hear them
cheering
you on.

When Dreams Feel Past Due

One day I was told my
smile has healing powers;
perhaps, it heals me
more so than you.

Alexis Harris

Trying to describe everything
you are and everything you're
capable of doing is like trying
to describe everything inside
the oceans or galaxies.

When Dreams Feel Past Due

When they called
I was elated;
and though
the calls stopped
I'm still worthy
of being celebrated.

-Gatekeepers

Alexis Harris

Forgive yourself,
then release yourself
from yourself.

When Dreams Feel Past Due

Last night,
He wrapped
a special gift and boxed it
inside my television.
He kissed my cheeks as the
screen waved farewell;
Until next time, I said.
He nodded in reassurance
of a "next time."

Today,
He wrapped a special gift
and boxed it inside my lungs.
He walked each breath down
the aisle of my body as my soul
made vows to Him for the 24th
year in a row.

-Happy Birthday

Alexis Harris

If the rainbow you're
following doesn't
have a pot of gold
at the end of it,
you're following
the wrong rainbow.

When Dreams Feel Past Due

It's mesmerizing to think
I'm still here though I haven't
the slightest idea of what I'm
doing.

-Green

Alexis Harris

Rest assured you're exactly
where you're supposed
to be.

When Dreams Feel Past Due

The things we need always
find their way to us.

Alexis Harris

My soul is a tree—grounded
and rooted and still standing.

When Dreams Feel Past Due

Even if my soul fails to
remember, my heart will
never forget how kind
you've been.

Alexis Harris

THEN COMES MARRIAGE

When Dreams Feel Past Due

I saw a garden.
You saw a cemetery.
We were looking at the
same thing.

-Views

Alexis Harris

I'd rather have love
than make love.

When Dreams Feel Past Due

I blamed you for wanting
to take advantage of me—
the truth is, I was just
mad you got to me before
I got to you.

Alexis Harris

When you're used to hurting,
healing feels like an abuse lover.

When Dreams Feel Past Due

My soul envied the way
you captivated my body
and conformed it to yours.

Alexis Harris

In that moment, you sent a
shock through my body;
that's when exhilaration
and exhaustion
became indistinguishable.

When Dreams Feel Past Due

My smile caresses my
face though you no
longer caress me.

Alexis Harris

I will release you
knowing that in
due time you will
come full circle.

When Dreams Feel Past Due

Your pen sketched
an interpretation
of me I never
thought possible.

-Beholder

Alexis Harris

Don't leave. But if
you do, don't come back.

-Salty

When Dreams Feel Past Due

The bees made love to
the flowers and the aroma
of their passion sent my
nostrils to Heaven.

Alexis Harris

I know you didn't hurt me
on purpose. Or maybe you did.
Either way, I have no choice
but to get through this.

When Dreams Feel Past Due

My womanhood birthed in
me the strength your manhood
castrated from you.

Alexis Harris

My heart was weak
not because you
left, but because you
didn't say bye.

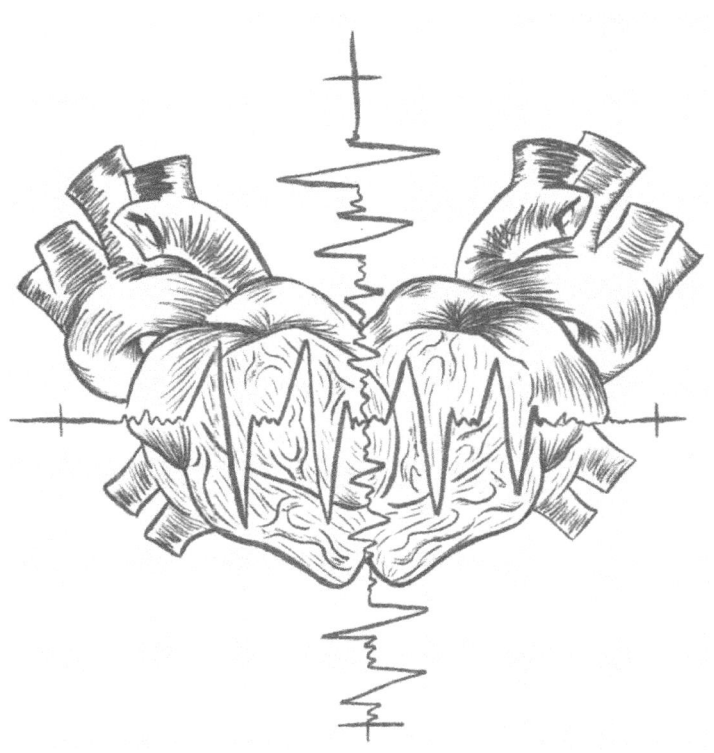

When Dreams Feel Past Due

I said I wasn't hungry.
Not only did you convince
me I was, you convinced me
to crave you.

Alexis Harris

You were my reason
to rise and the reason
I fell.

When Dreams Feel Past Due

I tell myself I want
to be alone so that
you never have the
power to make
me be alone.

Alexis Harris

I'd never do to you
what you did to me.
You're far too weak
and that'd be far too
cruel.

When Dreams Feel Past Due

I want to have my
cake and eat yours,
too.

Alexis Harris

In that moment,
my eyes undressed you;
my mind pulled out its
tape recorder and kept
your voice on repeat;
then, my heart became
predator and you, prey.

When Dreams Feel Past Due

I wanted you to
want me, but I
didn't even want
me.

-Double Standards

Alexis Harris

I pity the rain and
how it's forced to obey
the skies. I pity the
rain and how its path
is determined by the
winds. I pity the rain
because it reflects me—
and the skies and wind
reflect you.

When Dreams Feel Past Due

Love is a universal language
in which you aren't fluent.

Alexis Harris

Oh, how I long to converse
with you and absorb the ancestral
stories of triumph planted in the soil
of your soul which causes your spine to
erect itself with pride.

-Mother Nature

When Dreams Feel Past Due

I desired nothing more
than to dwell with you
for a momentary embrace.
Just as my spirit relaxed
itself into your arms, my
body trembled at your majesty.

-Little Spoon

Alexis Harris

You asked what tugged
at my heartstrings as you
held me like a ventriloquist.

When Dreams Feel Past Due

I sought refuge in
your form of rebellion.

-Our Relationship Was Doomed

Alexis Harris

The truth is, you can't
make me stay, but you can't
make me leave either.

-I Love You

When Dreams Feel Past Due

You left me at the altar
but my finger and her ring
continued to exchange vows.
I looked down in despair at
how he tightly caressed her
and tore their embrace in a
desperate attempt to save her.

Alexis Harris

I was intrigued because
you were a good salesman;
and Lord knows I'm a
sucker for discounts.

When Dreams Feel Past Due

The tape recorder of
my mind replays your
words like a broken record—
but the words weren't yours.
They were mine.
I spoon-fed you like a child
because I knew if I gave
you a moment to speak,
your first word would be
goodbye.

Alexis Harris

I placed the blame on
you because it was much
too heavy for me.

When Dreams Feel Past Due

I wanted to fall,
you forced me to stand.
I hated you, then.
I love you, now.

-Hindsight

Alexis Harris

You disguised your
desires in a recipe book;
but, honey, I'm no chef.

When Dreams Feel Past Due

I'm sorry for thinking
my happiness could be
found in you. That pressure
was much too great—
I would've ran, too.

Alexis Harris

I trusted you,
but you didn't
trust you;
and that was
enough
for me.

When Dreams Feel Past Due

Don't you dare
think less
of me because my
life hasn't been
as action-packed
as you'd like.
Don't you dare
let this smile fool you.

Alexis Harris

For everything there
is a season;
all things are
made beautiful
in time;
for everything
there is a season;
I think you
skipped mine.

When Dreams Feel Past Due

I wanted you; but
I was over you by
the time you wanted me.

-Too Little Too Late

Alexis Harris

We need each
other; don't
be stubborn
for too long.

When Dreams Feel Past Due

I walked in the bedroom
of your life and you were
sound asleep. I was wide awake
and didn't want to slumber—
you hated that about me.

-When Dreams Lie Dormant

Alexis Harris

We mourn what was and
what could've been far more
than we accept and
appreciate what is.

When Dreams Feel Past Due

You knew everything
about me; and still
chose me.

Alexis Harris

You covered me
but it felt like
I was being
smothered.
Sure I could breathe
but only short
gasps; and
while that seems
sufficient, I
needed a deep inhale.

When Dreams Feel Past Due

I'm done trying to
get people to support;
my magic isn't in their
approval, like, comment,
or share.

It's in the curve of
my smile, the bend of my hips,
the texture of my hair.
The spark in my eyes?
That's where the magic lies.

And whether you approve
of me or not, I've got everything,
everyone,
every sound,
every drum,
stepping to
my own beat.

The path I journey
is up to me.
You follow.
I lead?
It's not necessary.
You know right from wrong.
You were raised well, remember?

Alexis Harris

We're all given the
same 365 days;
January through December.
I can't spend my time
waiting on support—
because people like you
don't want to help build,
bake, or ice the cake...
but swear you
deserve the
first cut.

-An Ode to Dr. Maya Angelou

When Dreams Feel Past Due

I kissed a snake;
he promised not
to bite... but he
lied and disappeared
like a thief in the
night.

Alexis Harris

Anything was possible;
but nothing happened.

When Dreams Feel Past Due

Put your ego
aside and go.

Alexis Harris

I don't trust
people who don't
dance—so,
please dance.

When Dreams Feel Past Due

People are the single
best and worst
thing to ever
happen to the
world,
in the world,
and for the world;
but without
them the world
would lose its heartbeat
and would exist
no more.

Alexis Harris

THEN COMES A BABY

When Dreams Feel Past Due

It takes guts to conceive dreams
in your spirit knowing your
soul will instantly fall in
love with something your
body may never birth.

Alexis Harris

"I'm tired of waiting"—
my heart sobbed.
"Imagine how we feel!"
my angels replied.

When Dreams Feel Past Due

The pain was in preparation
for the joy; and the idea of joy
made the pain more bearable.

-Cycles

Alexis Harris

Your laughter teaches
my heart to embrace a
sound foreign to my ears.

When Dreams Feel Past Due

If you force your dream out
of its womb prematurely
you'll birth something
that's malnourished.

Alexis Harris

When you look and feel like you've
gained weight, remember you're
carrying the heaviness of the
dreams inside of you.

When Dreams Feel Past Due

Notions of good and bad
depend on who you ask.

Alexis Harris

Make mistakes—
for those coming
after you will
be grateful.

When Dreams Feel Past Due

It's one thing when you
can prepare for the pain;
it's an entirely different
story when you can't.

-Brace Yourself

Alexis Harris

Rain is necessary
for growth;
as is sunshine.

When Dreams Feel Past Due

...in due time.

-Note to Self

Alexis Harris

Don't be afraid
of new adventures;
we're nomads
by nature.

When Dreams Feel Past Due

Loss is a part of life;
gain is, too.

Alexis Harris

We were given tear ducts
because our maker knew
we'd need a good release
every now and then.

When Dreams Feel Past Due

You told me to
stop smiling;
I didn't even realize
I was smiling.

Alexis Harris

You are beautiful.
This is your time.
Be a star.
You're in the wrong place.
Your fragrance gives you away.

When Dreams Feel Past Due

The ultrasound of my spirit
just revealed the womb of my
soul is housing twins. The first
round of birthing will be for me.
The second for you.

Alexis Harris

I'm not asking you to be fearless;
I'm asking you to be brave.

When Dreams Feel Past Due

IN A BABY CARRIAGE

Alexis Harris

You could pay me
for every tear;
but you'd go bankrupt
paying for the laughs—
for the laughs
never end;
the tears always do.

When Dreams Feel Past Due

Sure the rain may come back,
but let's enjoy the sunshine
for the time being.

Alexis Harris

The trees must have
conversations for days
and stories for centuries.

When Dreams Feel Past Due

Finding happiness in every moment
guarantees the fleeting feeling
will return even if it fades.

Alexis Harris

Life is to be lived—
not endured.

When Dreams Feel Past Due

You are everything you
want to be already.

Alexis Harris

Sharing, in all its forms,
is therapeutic – and nothing
you give is ever wasted.

When Dreams Feel Past Due

Somewhere along the line
we decided to demonize
natural and idolize plastic.

Alexis Harris

Dreaming isn't as hard
as believing; and believing
isn't as hard as working.

When Dreams Feel Past Due

All of life is a series
of wishing, working,
and waiting.

Alexis Harris

You can dream more than
one dream at a time.

-No Limit

When Dreams Feel Past Due

Inner beauty is
to outer beauty
what an engine
is to a car;
a necessity.

Alexis Harris

I was pleased to believe
in the universe.
But then I met
its creator.

When Dreams Feel Past Due

"What are you doing here?"
the Body says to its Spirit.
*"And how long are you
here to dwell?"*

*"I existed before my
occupancy with you;
and as far as my stay?
Only time will tell."*
the Spirit replies.

At this point the soul
jumps in; injecting its
personality.
*"I'll be your mind, will,
emotions...until you
return to eternity."*

"So I've been here before?"
the Body cries.

Its spirit and soul smirk
with joy in their eyes.

*"Oh what majesty awaits
you on the other side."*

Alexis Harris

Everything feels so familiar.
I've been here before.

-Deja Vu

When Dreams Feel Past Due

Don't reserve today's happiness
for tomorrow's possibilities.

Alexis Harris

Trees are our ancestors' way
of showing us that all is
forgiven. Watch as they grow
together – their unity on full
display.

When Dreams Feel Past Due

Before time began, we existed
in eternity with God
our creator – no wonder
we have creative souls.

Alexis Harris

The only thing I
know for sure
is what I don't.

When Dreams Feel Past Due

If we were feet
we'd be the soles
on which the world
rests its crooked toes.

Alexis Harris

We can't forget:
we mustn't allow
anyone to make us forget.
We can't accept one
or two exceptions
to the rule as some
grandiose display of regret.

When Dreams Feel Past Due

Never equate followers
with talent.

Alexis Harris

I don't care
to have everything
the light touches
so long as I possess
the light that
touches everything.

When Dreams Feel Past Due

No questions
are stupid;
not even the ones
you already know
the answer to.

Alexis Harris

Even the darkest
storms have lightning;
use it to see your
way clear.

When Dreams Feel Past Due

Wishing on stars
became futile
when my Father
told me He
created them.

Alexis Harris

We're all trying to
figure it out; no one
has done so already.

When Dreams Feel Past Due

Comfort zones
can easily
become prisons—
be careful.

Alexis Harris

I blew out a candle
tonight and though
its light dimmed
I saw its smoke rise
and so too
our spirits leave
their bodies
only to mix and
mingle in the skies.

When Dreams Feel Past Due

Though life is rough
it's worth living—
I looked back over
the years and
saw many moments
where I didn't even
realize I was smiling;
but I was.

Alexis Harris

Life is a journey and we're all new to this.
Along the way, you'll laugh, cry, love, hate, hurt,
survive, hope, dream, and—above all else—thrive.
The locket of your heart houses a fire that burns
much brighter than you know. May that fire
be the light you carry on this expedition.
You will need it. Light up the skies with your
brilliance, radiate beyond
galaxies, and blaze a trail like none other
on a path that is uniquely yours. Thank
you for following mine.

-Lex

When Dreams Feel Past Due

Alexis Harris is an African American creative visionary who loves God and loves people.

-About the Author

Alexis Harris

Dear dreamers, you are a special breed.
You will get through this
and it will be glorious.

-About the Book

www.ingramcontent.com/pod-product-compliance
Lightning Source LLC
Chambersburg PA
CBHW020929090426
42736CB00010B/1085